Copyright©2020 ARNOLD KUNTZ PH.D

CONTENTS

INTRODUCTION

The increase and advancement in the healthcare system have increased the chance of healthcare business. Many public and private hospitals are running these days and fulfilling's the needs of the society and generating income. Still, the need for more hospitals and healthcare services are increasing day by day. Specialized hospitals in any medical field are also working in the health care industry like children hospitals etc. Healthcare industry is also becoming selective in the hiring of new employees as they are focusing on trained and specialized staff for the hospital. Starting a hospital is a good idea and a secure investment. However, you should develop a proposal for the hospital business. The OGS capital would guide you develop and compressive business scheme for you. You would also need a license to start a hospital business and must decide a niche in which you are interested in working which can be a children hospital, orthopedic hospital or general hospital. You must also understand the requirements of the community you are interested in starting a hospital.

WHY TO HIRE OUR SERVICES?

A hospital business is a technical venture and need planning and strategy. You can't merely buy a place and hire doctors to start this venture. You must know the number of the people you are targeting for the hospital because it will help to develop the strategy. It is important to take advice and help from the experts so that you won't ignore the basic issues. You may forget to understand potential threats, demands, and weakness of your business. OGS capital would help you to develop a good proposal and help you to attract investors. We will highlight your strengths and minimize potential threats. OGS capital would ensure confidentially of your information and take all precautionary measures to make you satisfy. The primary goal of OGS capital is to write a valuable proposal within your estimated budget.

GOALS OF THE OGS CAPITAL

OGS capital utilizes the services of experts that help you design the proposal according to your customized needs and goals. Some aims and goals for your hospital business plan are given below:

1. Writing and developing an attainable and feasible vision and mission for your venture.

2. Analyzing of the current market trends for your healthcare venture.

3. Formulating and writing a plan with the consolation of the experts.

4. Helps you to decide niche for your healthcare business after analysis of the market demand.

5. Recommend the good business locations.

6. Assists in developing effective financial strategies for your healthcare venture.

7. Development of marketing and advertisement strategy which is also cost effective.

8. Development of expanding strategy of your venture.

The proposal gives you an idea about how would you start your venture and attract investors for the potential healthcare venture. Starting a healthcare venture in a complicated and yet sophisticated process so you need to spend time, energy and money in developing the proposal. You might think of yourself an expert in business planning, but you may ignore some of the facts in writing the proposal. OGS capital service would help you to write a good proposal for you and your company.

REGULATORY REQUIREMENTS FOR STARTING A HOSPITAL BUSINESS

Hospitals play a crucial role in providing health services in communities and in the nation as a whole. From routine services like medical check-up, drug prescription, child delivery to more complex services like transplants, fertility treatments etc, hospitals quickly remind us that "health is wealth". However, because of the sensitive nature of the hospital business, it is important to comply with regulatory requirements when venturing into the hospital business environment.

The regulatory requirements for starting a hospital business in Nigeria include:

Licences/Permits

1. Business Registration: It is necessary that you begin by registering your business with the Corporate Affairs Commission (CAC).

2. Practising License: All hospitals are expected to have a practising license which is authorised by Medical and Dental Council of Nigeria (MDCN) and is subject to annual

renewal.

3. Authorization: The Federal Ministry of Health will have to confirm that you have the required qualifications that give you the legal right to operate a hospital in Nigeria.

Educational Qualifications/ Staffing
1. Doctors: He/ she should possess a minimum educational qualification of Bachelor of Medicine and Bachelor of Surgery (MBBS), and must have completed his/ her medical internship programme.

2. Nurses: He/ she should be a Registered Nurse with the Nursing and Midwifery Council of Nigeria (NMCN). According to NMCN, any registered and properly trained nurse with a minimum of five years working experience can set up a hospital to handle only minor cases.

3. Staffing: The significance of employing the right staff cannot be over emphasized. In Lagos for instance, qualified professionals required to be employed in your hospital include:

• One Medical Practitioner in-charge with a minimum of 5 years post qualification experience.

• One Medical Practitioner per shift.

• One Registered Nurse in-charge of Nursing Services.

• One Registered Staff Nurse/Midwife or Staff Nurse per 8 in-patients beds per shift.

• One Laboratory Assistant/Technician.

• One Registered Pharmacist for a Hospital/Pharmacy Technician.

- Medical Records and Secretarial Staff.

- Ward Assistant or Aides (optional).

INFRASTRUCTURAL REQUIREMENTS

The minimum basic facility requirements according to the Health Facility Monitoring and Accreditation Agency (HEFAMAA) include.

BUILDING

Your building which must be composite not forming part of normal residential accommodation must have:

For Out-Patient

• Waiting / reception room of 4x3 meters with sitting facilities, registration table.

• Medical record facilities.

• Consulting room (s) of 4x3 meters with examination couches wash-hand basin, towels and basic diagnostic tools.

• Treatment room of 4x3 metres with Instrument / drug cabinet, pedal bin and wash-hand basin and towels.

• Toilet facilities with water closet.

• Staff / cloak room.

• Dispensing room with pharmacy technician dispensing if compounding a registered Pharmacist is required.

• Oxygen cylinder with gauge and mask and suction machine.

• Other services - ambulance and fire extinguisher.

For In-Patient

• Lying-in ward with minimum distance of one meter between two adjoining beds of 1x3 metres between two rows of beds.

• Ward(s) with locker and over-bed table for each bed (separate Rooms for male and female patients).

• Delivery rooms (where applicable) of 12 sq. meters.

• First stage labour room (where applicable).

• Suitably equipped theatre with floor to ceiling ceramic tiling.

• Sluice room.

• Toilet facilities - 1 water closet per 8 beds (separate for male and female).

• Bathroom facilities - 1 bathroom per 8 beds (separate for male and female).

• Nurse bay.

EQUIPMENT

Your hospital facility is expected to be equipped amongst others with:

• Adequate and suitable theatre equipment/instruments for minor/ major surgeries.

• Suction machine

• Oxygen cylinder with gauge and mask

• Anaesthetic machine (arrangement with Anaesthetist may be made to provide when needed

• Operating lamp

• Adequate delivery/ labour room equipment.

Other minimum facility requirements according to HEFAMAA include:
• Clean and adequate water supply pipe borne, borehole water tank

• Washable floors

• Adequate drainage

• Adequate ventilation

• Adequate illumination.

• Laundry

• Kitchen

ARNOLD KUNTZ PH.D

• Fire extinguisher

16

HEALTH REGULATORY AUTHORITIES IN NIGERIA

Health regulatory authorities in Nigeria have been put in place to ensure the quality, safety, and efficacy of all clinical establishments in the country. According to the Federal Ministry of Health, the authorized health regulatory bodies in Nigeria among others include:

• Medical and Dental Council of Nigeria (MDCN)

• Nursing and Midwifery Council of Nigeria (NMCN)

• Pharmacist Council of Nigeria (PCN)

Each state in the country has its own regulatory body for monitoring health facilities in its state. In Lagos state for instance, the Health Facility Monitoring and Accreditation Agency (HEFAMAA) have been positioned to ensure that health facilities meet required standard.

In conclusion, it is paramount when starting a hospital business that you comply with regulatory requirements so that you are in a position to offer quality healthcare services.

HEALTHCARE BUSINESS MODEL AND HOSPITAL BUSINESS PLAN TEMPLATE

FEATURES OF HEALTHCARE BUSINESS AND ITS IMPORTANCE

The business of hospitals and health care organizations is one of the most emerging industries and globally adopted by people from all over the world. It is a profitable as well as long term stable business. As we know, health is an essential need of the society. Hence, the importance of health management services and organization can never be underestimated. Starting a healthcare institute and organization require a proper and reliable template or proposal. This is a layout proposal which describes the basis policy, construction, and needs of a health care organization

Starting a new Healthcare venture requires a thorough understanding of the national or government as well as public policy. You need to understand how people deal with the matters related to health and what their requirements are. You need to set up your healthcare system which can also be a hospital according to the prevailing trends of a society in which you are starting your new health management and caring venture. Below is the sample proposal or a sample template for your prospective venture.

SAMPLE HEALTHCARE BUSINESS PLAN

The business proposal is the document that elaborates the structure of the potential venture. Let's start with a brief overview of the industry before moving to sample healthcare business plan:

HEALTHCARE INDUSTRY OVERVIEW

Health care services and new hospitals are one of the fastest expanding industries in the world. Its growth depends upon the needs of society. The wealth and development of a nation are dependent upon its health. Healthcare service providers or organizations are a very serious concern in every part of the world. In fact, healthcare industry consumes a vast amount of a country's budget because providing best health care services to people is the most important task. Every government ensures that its citizens get the best healthcare services possible.

A source that can provide health care services is only a proficient health care provider that may be a doctor, a nurse or an organization itself. Hospitals, health care clinics, and health centers all are the sources of a healthy nation. They serve their duties and provide their best services to ensure the healthy environment for the people. In fact, the environment around people is made by the society. A healthy society means that the people living in it enjoy best health services.

Different operators operate a medical institute or

hospital. These operators can be general medical facility providers or the hospitals that re-licensed from government and are of required standards according to the government policies. These health care provider centers and hospitals provide different medical as well as diagnostic treatments to the patients. These patients are provided best services like pharmacy, operational treatments, surgical handlings and general and special wards and rooms.

There are many large health care organizations in all over the world which provide international standard healthcare services to the people all around the world. United Nation's Institute WHO provides about 19400 thousand nurses, 9200 thousand general physicians, about 1900 thousand dentists, about 1300 thousand general health workers, and about 2600 thousand pharmacists worldwide. These records are the proof that health industry or healthcare business services are the largest business field all over the world.

In 2011, US spent about 17.9 of its GDP rate on hospitals, health care units, nursing workshops, laboratories, diagnostic centers, pharmacists, health care systems and industries providing surgical and medical instruments industries which can be stated as a world record of the USA in the world. Many experts and analysts reported that in 2016 the share of health care systems in the GDP reached 19.6% for the US.

Starting a new hospital requires a lot of hard work. There are many requirements that should be first completed for starting a new hospital. Investing in hospitals and health care business requires some completion of local and federal laws. These laws are passed to ensure adequate medical services, equipment, and functional policies. Maintenance of operational records, accidental services, finalizing rates and environmental protection are some factors which are regulated by state healthcare policy. If you can formulate and regulate these policies in your proposal, then you are close to establishing a large profitable and reliable venture.

HOSPITAL BUSINESS PLAN TEMPLATE

The sample Healthcare Business Plan should contain the following:

Market Analysis

A complete market analysis can offer you a huge chain of progress stream. Market analysis captures the facts of the market for the healthcare industry. The hospital can use these facts for the progressive development of its policies. Hence a thorough market analysis can change the organization's trends. Market analysis is a market like market forecast and can help the industry to project its future growth and estimated budget. Market analysis offer two-dimensional predictions that are market trends and market targets. OGS capital services will help you develop and write the research based market analysis that would help you to understand current market trends.

Market Trends

Indeed hospital is a vast industry which offers much commercial as well as professional hard work. The hospital industry provides many services which are essential for a smooth living society. Hospital is a part of our community, and without the hospital, the trends of society are heavily stormed. But this huge hospital market is also dependent upon some gigantic and multi-dimensional patterns. These multi-dimensional trends are known as market trends. Market trends develop a specific culture for the progress of a hospital industry. Usually, a hospital works in providing external health care, and they take care of the physical body. This body is the primary constructor of hospital mechanism.

The market trends affect hospital directly and indirectly. These market trends are so vast that every field of the hospital is nested in them. For example, latest technology medical equipment is obtained from technical medical industry which is another market. Similarly, petrol used in ambulances, medicines used in injections and drips, drugs given to the patients, surgical instruments used in surgical operations, building materials for building development, electricity used for general use and even jobs are related to the markets which control the hospital venture.

So in order to handle and manage these multi-trends, a hospital industry always tries to organize its potential in the direction of the market trends. A marketing organizer and sales manager of a hospital industry always assure to regulate the policy trend in the market track. Hence Market trends of society are the basic factors that can either develop a industry or destroy it in a disastrous way. So a complete over look on these trends is required to ensure a progressive long term development.

Market to be targeted

Market effects hospital in many directions but the goal of every hospital industry is to catch the top market opportunities. Every hospital in the industry wants to progress collectively which means that every health care or hospital organization's first goal is to develop itself by all means. But for this, it has to work in the direction of the market. We can say that a hospital in the industry can only progress and develop if it establishes a mainstream contact with the market trends. A developed hospital always works together with the main market and hospital's team can only make relationship with the market by following the trends of the industry. This is what the responsibility of the marketing manager is.

Competitive industry

A hospital industry is a very broad term which is why organizers or managers of these industries always try to compete with each other. We can say that if you are starting a hospital organization, this means that you are participating in a well-broad international contest. To compete with other industries, the basic rule is to develop your own services and start working with a progressing approach. The another way to compete in the contest of international approach is to fully understand the needs of the clients and satisfy them by providing them experienced professional services, and this can only be done by hiring experienced and qualified staff. You must also train the new employees by taking them in the conferences and offering them professional meetings.

HOSPITAL BUSINESS MODEL

The hospital business plan template should contain the hospital business model which is described in detail below:

The hospital business model will contain the services provided by the hospital along with detailed description of the duties all the staff members will perform.

SERVICES TO BE PROVIDED IN HOSPITAL

To start a certified and licensed slandered health care hospital we should ensure that international standard facilities should be provided to the patients like X-ray, laser diagnostic and other imaging services, Clinical and health care laboratories for diagnostic facilities, operational and surgical wards and rooms services, Inpatient services, outpatient facilities and other medical services. You should also facilitate patients with well trained, fully equipped highly certified doctors and staff. You should determine adequate working timings and 24 hours duty timings for an emergency ward whole week. You should have well operated and trained calling services and health workers facilities. Your staff and doctors must cooperate with the culture requirements so that the customers can properly explain their needs. You should ensure first class management for the customers.

You should ensure that the customers of your hospital are well treated. Your services must consist professional and well-trained doctors, specialists, dentists, nurses, opticians, management chancellor for mental health, general medication chancellor, health workers, and general physical therapists.

Your hospital should offer basic services and facilities like imaging diagnostic services, emergency healthcare facilities for emergency injury management, medical laboratory services, disease recognizing services, etc.

STAFF REQUIRED FOR THE HOSPITAL AND THEIR DUTIES

The structure of hospital business plan must have a solid and firm foundation base. You must hire and recruit certified professionals including doctors, nurses, dentists, management councilors, speech, physical and occupational therapists, workers for emergency management or in complicated job positions of your hospital or health care organization. Hiring and recruiting only specialized and well-qualified employees in your organization is not only essential for providing high-quality service but also important for increasing your credibility for the clients. Hiring certified doctors are also important for following the regulations of the state. These factors can build your hospital and healthcare organization as a globally recognized hospital. For hiring a new applicant, you should not only judge his / her qualification and experience, but also he/she should also be honest, authentic, straightforward and nice with customers. He/she should be ready to deal and help the owner in developing the venture. As a profitable venture is the fruit of high performance of management, so sharing responsibilities with the employees and managers will

ARNOLD KUNTZ PH.D

help you in developing your hospital in the industry.

DUTIES AND RESPONSIBILITIES

Some job positions in a large health care organizations already working in the industry are Chief of medical management, Doctor, Surgeon, Dentist, Nurse, Admin Manager, Information Technologist, Pharmacist, Marketing Manager, Account Manager/Accountant, Customer Care Manager, and Cleaners. Let us analyze their duties and tasks they will perform in detail.

CHIEF OF MEDICAL MANAGEMENT

Chief medical management is accountable for providing a track and direction for management of health care venture. Chief of medical management is responsible for sharing, designing and implementing the vision and mission of health care organization or hospital according to the existing industry. Chief medical management also leads the progress and development of the hospital's strategy. Chief medical management advises and supervises the cases of severe medical and high profile patients and clients. Chief of medical management is also responsible for transactions and dealings of contracts, recruitment of positions and managing salaries. Chief of medical management also supervises the contracts and signs dealing transactions for the new hospital or healthcare organization in the industry. The team also documents the growth and progress of the hospital.

DOCTOR

The responsibility of the doctor is to provide specialized medical facilities to the clients. A doctor offers physical, vocal and occupational therapies. The doctor also handles and manages medical and clinical emergencies.

PHARMACIST

The Pharmacist handles the routine functionalities of the hospital dispensary store. He or she also provides guidance on health and fitness issues, describes symptoms and explain directions of medicines. The Pharmacist handles the recruiting, teaching and training the management staff for the hospital pharmacy. A Pharmacist processes and manages the prescriptions of medication issues. The pharmacist is accountable for administering the medicine stock and also sell the medicines to the customer along with ordering the drugs. Pharmacist arranges and participates in professional meetings with different medical representatives. The pharmacist manages the products and materials. Pharmacist deals with marketing services and participates in the third party meetings too. The pharmacist is also responsible for managing the tasks which are appointed by the director of the medical office.

NURSES

They are responsible for handling the patients and managing particular injury situations. Nurses are also accountable for offering complete medication courses and other managing services. Nurses support and help the doctors in handling the treatment of the patient.

MANAGER OF THE MARKETING DEPARTMENT

Marketing manager handles researches and organizes internal as well as external statistical information, by comparing it with other competitors in the industry, in order to develop the hospital by identifying the market needs of the clients to attract them. Marketing manager identifies as well as design the development of contracts and deals. Marketing manager designs the structure of financial programs of the hospital. Sales manager also guarantees the achievements of these programs. A marketing manager documents the proposals assigns the rates and finalizes the financial strategies of the hospital. He/she manages the market researches and also conducts market analyses. He/she also studies the possibilities of extreme conditions for the hospital. Marketing manager also manages the administration of the development programs and also locate the trends of market needs and identify the customer's requirements. Sales manager also designs new programs and execute them for increasing the hospital income. He/she also develops new ways of improving and expanding the health care organization. Marketing Manager motivates and addresses the team to exceed the required targets for the development of hospital.

INFORMATION TECHNOLOGIST

Information technologist is an IT specialist who operates the website and software of the organization as per the latest trends in the industry. Information technologist manage the e-commerce characteristics of hospital and health care organization. Information technologist is also accountable for the maintenance of the computer and software used in the organization. They also update the computers according to the needs of the hospital. They handle the web servers, websites, data entry software, and operating systems of the hospital computers. In fact the primary duty of information technician is to handle and manage different computer and IT related tasks and resolve any issues that arise for the organization.

ACCOUNT MANAGER

Account Manager or Accountant is responsible for managing the economic reports, budget related documents and monetary accounts for the hospital and health care organization. Accountants analyze the financial possibilities and sources for the development of new projects for the hospital and health care organization to gain a better position in the industry. Account Manager conducts general market surveys to analyze the upcoming trends of industry. Therefore, the accountant is accountable for the forecast of monetary risks for the hospital. Accountant acts as a manager of cash department and uses his or her experience in accounting financial documents and analyzing the results of analysis. Accountant develops new economic and financial management plans for the policy structure. Account Manager administrates the payrolls. An accountant is responsible for ensuring obedience in legal taxation on behalf of hospital. The accountant develops the policies of financial contracts with the marketing manager of the hospital.

CUSTOMER SERVICE MANAGER

Customer services executive or manager is responsible for welcoming new customers, greeting them via any source of communication like telephone, e-mail, or on any social network, providing them any related information and leading them to facilities if required. Service manager ensures contacts with the clients through SMS, e-mail or phone. Service Manager provides best professional client services and facilitates them through service manager experience. A customer service manager plays a very vital role in the development of any organization in any industry like hospital and health care institutes. Service manager uses best means to facilitate the clients and use his/her experiences to attract customers. Client services manager interacts with the customers and explains prospects of the hospital organization to build the customer's interest in the hospital's services. Service managers also manage the tasks given by the director of creative sources in the required time efficiently. Customer service manager is also responsible for advertising the characteristics of the organization's new projects, products, and services. Service managers start new campaigns for spreading advertisements about the helpful materialistic information about the hospital's facilities.

CLEANERS

Cleaners are responsible and accountable for the cleaning and dusting the hospital building and facilities all time. They are also responsible for ensuring that any kind of supplies like drinking water, dustbins and toiletries don't expire or run out. Cleaners clean the internal as well as external facilities of the hospital. They are also responsible for cleaning the hospital's grounds and gardens. They manage every task that is given by the administration or HR manager.

SWOT ANALYSIS

SWOT analysis is an important part to be written in the healthcare venture plan. It gives concrete idea about the strengths, weakness, threats and opportunities of your potential venture. Analysis of threats would help to develop pre-planned strategy about how to deal with the potential risks.

a) Strength: The hospital in health care industry will be strengthened by the overall professional strategies. Well certified professionals including doctors, nurses, dentists and even managers play key roles in the development and progress of hospital and health care organization. We can say that the professionals of a hospital or health care organization are the center of development for the hospital. Location of the hospital is still another center of importance. If the hospital is in the central position of a state, then the importance of the hospital will be also be magnified and focused. A central place or location means where the clients or customers can easily and quickly reach the organization. A central position may be a capital of population or critical state of a country. So a central location can centralize a new hospital joining the healthcare industry. Also, the working hours of the hospital must be suitable for the clients with especially the emergency unit working 24 hours a day and seven days a week. Easy payment methods, latest equipped medical assistance, a professional customer service and cultural characteristics make an organization a central institute.

b) Weaknesses: Weaknesses are the faults and ignored facts in the proposal. Weaknesses of a hospital can be diminished by assisting a professional venture supervisor. Over viewing the hospital proposal can also decrease the faulty holes in the strategy of a hospital.

c) Threats: The major threat to other businesses is the financial fall or exhaustion of all available funds. This can affect the general working of the hospital and ultimately can cause complete failure of your venture. These threats can be removed by recognizing them earlier and by thorough workout on the policies.

d) Opportunities: Opportunities of hospital or health care organization depend upon the development field of services. The hospital organization opportunities are directly linked to the opportunities that your organization provides. A hospital venture can offer you a complete vast field chains. In short, you can develop your hospital by creating chains, in this way you can multiply your progress easily. This is an immense opportunity that a hospital venture offers you.

SALES AND MARKETING STRATEGY.

1. Source of income. You should understand and propose your source of income in the hospital business plan. You should generate your income with the legal framework and with your services. You may generate income from inpatient and outpatient care, laboratory services, income through operation and surgery, psychological services and personal injury care.

2. Marketing Strategy and Sales Strategy. Any hospital that really wants to work for the people and to stay in business should have a well thought out marketing and sales strategy. So this is a very important part of the hospital business plan. When you are beginning a hospital venture, you would want to establish long-term relationships with all your customers, and you want them to consider you a reliable source to come back to whenever they can, to ensure that you first have to devise a marketing and sales strategy that attract clients to your hospital.

Mention all the measures you will take to ensure this in

your healthcare business proposal. Tell a bit about your health care services and your customer service. Discuss any surveys or research material you used to calculate how to really get into the business effectively and strongly, and how you will be using your research to reach your target customers in a way that you make a long-term relationship with them. Write that what you want to do is to not only reach out to customers but to make sure that they stay loyal to you once they avail your services, and for that a great marketing strategy is needed. You can even take help from marketing experts for this part to really think out an effective marketing strategy that helps you reach out to the maximum number of potential customers and helps in increasing your sales by doing so.

Study the marketing strategies of other businesses in the healthcare industry, and develop your own, writing it down in this section of the business will really help in figuring out what you are planning to do and it will also show your potential investors that you are serious about this. Here is a bunch of stuff that you can do ensure you market to the maximum number of potential clients:

You can send introductory letters of your hospital to other business and corporate owners in your area.

Advertise through social media, newspapers, TV, etc.

You can list the hospital name in yellow pages which are local directories so everyone can look your name up.

Direct marketing can also be used and will be a good technique.

Do not forget to get people of credible nature to refer to your business to places they go to.

Whatever you think of doing of all these strategies write it down comprehensively in the marketing and sales strategy section.

SALE FORECASTS.

The sales forecast is an important point in the proposal. It is based on market survey. After a critical evaluation of the market, the chances to grow your business are quite high. However, you must forecast your business sales for atheist three years. Your sales in the starting year of the business may be up to approximately 100 thousand dollars from clients and you might get 250 thousand from health insurance firms. In the second year, it may be up to 250 thousand dollars from self and pay clients while 500 thousand dollars from health insurance firms. In the third year, sales forecast may be up to 500 thousand dollars from customers and 1500 thousand dollars from the health insurance companies. These forecasts are drawn from the available market trends. Economic recession may hamper the progress of the sales. It might be higher or lower in than expected. OGS capital services would help you to draw accurate estimated sales forecast.

PUBLICITY AND ADVERTISING STRATEGY

The next part of your business proposal is your publicity and advertising strategy, and publicity is the free content about your company that is advertised over the media, while the advertisement is the publishing you pay for. You will probably use both in order to promote your hospital venture, so you mention the publicity and advertising means and strategy you use in this section of the business proposal. The publicity and advertisement strategy helps promote your business to a vast audience, and in doing so it will also help you emerge out as one of the market leaders, and it will maximize all profitability factors.

You have to keep one thing in mind, the publicity and advertisement are not just a mean to bring people to your hospital, but it is also a way for you to tell everyone what your brand is about and how your business is different and what positive changes you will bring in the market. So think of all the conventional and non-conventional means that you can to publicize and advertise your business. This is a very important part, as this will be the first look of potential customers at your business, a good publicity and advertisement strategy can make or in some case break your business. Come up with it by putting a lot of thought into it and then document it effectively in the business proposal.

Here are some ways you can promote your brand in the public eye:
• Newspapers, magazines and social media platforms are the very basic places that you should definitely place advertisements on.

• You can also start by sponsoring some local events, this will be a very positive promotion.

• Place billboards in locations you know your primary audience will be.

• Put the business logo on company vehicles, they will act as a moving advertisement wherever they go.

• Make appealing flyers and distribute them locally.

PRICING STRATEGY

Once the advertising and marketing stage is one and people now know about your business the first thing they will ask will be how much they will be paying for your service. Devising a pricing strategy is a procedure that requires a lot of thought, you don't want to go too high so as to put off people, but you wouldn't want to sell your services for less either, finding the perfect balance is the key. Based on prices of your competitors, you need to come up with a pricing strategy that you think will deem good.

Next think of payment methods, like insurance, medicare, medicaid, whatever you use of these, think of reasons why you think customers would like using them first. Now that you know how the pricing goes and how payments will be made, put them in your business proposal, so potential investors know how much you will be charging, it is also a way for you to refer to and keep record once you start the hospital venture.

PAYMENT OPTIONS

In this day and age a number of payment options exist, try to include all these in your business, this is because different people find different options better for them and you need to cater to maximum people. Some options you can use for your hospital venture are:

- The conventional cash payment

- Usage of point of sale machines

- Mobile money is another popular method these days

- Online bank transfer

- Check payment

Consider these options and pick as many as you can, without any inconvenience. Mention these in your healthcare business proposal.

STARTUP EXPENDITURE-THE BUDGET REQUIRED

The establishment of hospital is not cheap that is why you have to make sure that you raise enough capital to cover all the expenses. You would need medical equipment which will need a large amount of investment.

You would need to cover some basic facilities which are mandatory for a hospital to run and without those facilities your hospital can't be considered as a standard medical facility. Without these facilities you may even be breaking some laws in some places. You would need the workforce from the general staff to nurses and doctors. This means it will take a huge chunk of investment to pay a large workforce. Medical equipment is also a necessity and unfortunately it is expensive. You would also have to pay the bills until you generate some revenue, and with all this you have to maintain a standard ambulance with quality equipment.

A general idea of things you would needing to start this business are listed below:

• Cost of registering a business

• Marketing of the business

• Legal expenses of the business

• The cost of recruiting a business consultant, you can have a contract based business consultant to lessen this cost.

• Cost of computer software like health monitoring software for critical patients etc.

• Insurance of the business

• Rent of the place in case you don't own the place

• Cost of storage hardware

• General starting expenses

• Cost of remodeling the building

• Cost of development of the website

• Cost of medical equipment and ambulance

• Cost of inventory at start

• Cost of furniture like tables, chairs, computers etc.

• Cost of drugs and drug supplies like injections, bandages etc; and cost of future drug supplies before the hospital is at breakeven

COVERING ALL THE COST AND EXPENSES

This business indeed needs a large investment that's why you need to make intelligent decisions while generating all that capital to earn revenue. Now the question remains what can be the sources which will generate the capital to be invested in the business. The answer to this is given by the following guidelines for people who are looking to establish a hospital. Here are the three ways to generate capital for investment:

First source:
The first source is your personal savings. You have to have personal savings to invest so that the pressure of generating capital from the rest of the two resources decreases. Also, this the only resource you are sure about beforehand that how much you will get to invest in the business.

Second resource:
The next resource is solely based on your social circle and your ability to convince people to join you in this venture. The second resource is the soft loans, which is the loans taken from family and friends. Communicate clearly and honestly to your friends and family to convince them to

join you.

Third resource:

Thirds resource is the loan from the bank.

THE STRATEGY FOR SUSTAINABILITY AND THE PLANNING TO EXPAND

Sustainability strategy and expansion proposal in the business plan not only depicts you as a person passionate about this venture but also, promotes confidence of the investor in you. The sustainability strategy and expansion proposal is also very important for the future of the business, without the goals set for the future the revenue generated will not increase and will not turn out to be a long term business venture.

The sustainability strategy of the hospital venture should focus on providing for the business and be at breakeven, that is the business won't need an external injection of capital. The next step is to generate more revenue than the cost that is at the stage of earning a profit.

Who will get the profit should also be discussed in the expansion proposal along with how the profit will be distributed among people. How much of the profit will be spent on further expansion and buying new equipment?

Sustainability strategy and expansion proposal are also

important because it attracts serious employees who dedicatedly work in their field. These workers are attracted to your business because they are looking for more opportunities and a long term setup to stay with the same hospital for a long period of time.

HOW OGS CAPITAL CAN HELP?

Since hospital businesses are not cheap and you need a large investment to establish it; it is very probable that among the three sources of capital, the personal saving and loan from bank will not be enough to cover all the cost.

Now when you are attracting investors you need a business proposal which will engage the investor and leave them is awe. More than often we see that a person with an innovative business idea can't turn it into reality they don't have enough capital to cover all the expenses and fail to get investors and when it comes to writing business proposal most of the people are at loss. The solution to this dilemma is OGS capital.

OGS Capital have the highly qualified and exceptionally skilled teams to handle your business plans for you. OGS Capital looks forward to facilitating the customer. If you are at loss on how to write the business plan for your business idea, then all you need to do is just place an order at OGS Capital. Placing an order is a piece of cake. You just give us a general idea of your business, and we will put our thinking hats on. If you even have a vague idea, discuss with our professional team to clarify the idea and place an order. We deliver with quality and speed. Only in 24 hours of placing the order we give you the business proposal.

Instead of following the templates available in the market our specialized team will start working on your business proposal. First a rough draft will be given to you so you can approve it and can tell us to modify it, if you want any changes. Shortly, after the approval of the draft, the business plan is given to you which will surely be attracting investors for your business.

SIX SECRETS TO RUNNING AN EFFECTIVE HOSPITAL

1. Make sure your records don't accumulate unwanted depreciation. If a piece of equipment or other asset is no longer in use, or in existence, it should be physically disposed of and removed from the books. For instance, if the hospital once owned a building and it wasn't remove from the records when it was replaced or sold, the hospital may have paid several years' worth of insurance on the old building. In addition to placing a strain on the hospital's finances, this carries accumulated depreciation on the hospital balance sheet making it appear older than it really is. Having fully depreciated assets, such as old MRIs, on the books make hospitals seem like they are dated and worn, you have to clean them out.

For one client, Principle Valuation identified $31 million in disposals to remove from the books, and almost all of it was fully depreciated. When the disposals are removed, the hospital's books more accurately reflected their real situation. Taking care of the books puts you in the best light.

The amount of expensed and accumulated depreciation effects a hospital's financial statements. For audit purposes it is important that processes and procedures are in place to maintain an accurate asset record. In addition, when hospital or health system executives are seeking debt financing, financial intermediaries, capital sources and rating agencies scrutinize the financial statements impacting the cost of capital and possibly access to capital.

2. Minimize staff turnover. Best practices across the board say that high staff turnover is bad for business because it takes time and energy to train employees, and losing their expertise is a drain on hospital resources. There are several reasons why a surgical hospital might have high turnover rates, including low employee satisfaction and higher wages at competing facilities. To meet these challenges head-on, hospital CEOs must have a sophisticated HR professional who is able to work with employees and executives to keep the turnover rate low.

3. Develop a strong managed care team. Failure to develop and utilize a well-managed care team is one of the most damaging practices when it comes to OR efficiency. If a surgical team is delayed from starting their next case because the anesthesiologist is still finishing up one patient or the next patient isn't ready for surgery, it creates an unnecessary roadblock that derails the surgical schedule and can leave both surgeons and patients dissatisfied. The concept of care team should also be extended to include a strategic partnership with OR leadership and care providers. For example, the anesthesia team can often partner with the OR circulating nurses to

streamline throughput and reduce redundant activities. A care team approach allows anesthesiologists and OR clinicians to coordinate patient care to optimize OR time.

4. Take control over the elements of competition that you can influence. There are certain competitive strategies that the hospital can't influence — including geography, demographics and payor competition — but they can influence the relationship between the hospital, payors and area physicians. Many times, this includes a physician-hospital alignment strategy. The hospital can also explore alignment with other tertiary providers in the community to provide a seamless continuum of care. All of this requires access to information across the continuum.

Additionally, hospital executives can influence how they develop the different departments. Many departments are modernized when the hospital partners with surgeons to perform new procedures, purchases new technology and updates data collection capabilities. Timely access to the right information is key, but don't forget to have the right human resources assets in place and the right people in leadership positions to focus on advancing care and improving the department's culture.

5. Conduct department evaluations before layoffs. One of the biggest mistakes hospitals can make when cutting jobs is establishing a fixed percentage cut in each department, according to Sherilynn Quist, workforce efficiency practice leader at management and consulting company Quorum Health Resources. This tactic may exacerbate staffing issues by eliminating positions in departments

that are understaffed, which may jeopardize quality and patient safety. It never works. "You'll end up right back [where you started]." Instead, she suggests using benchmarks and thorough evaluations of departments to identify areas where cuts would have the least negative impact or have a positive impact. "Understand what departments [you] can go after without affecting clinical quality or patient satisfaction.

6. Consider partnering with a BPO. When deciding on a Business Process Outsourcer, it's important to understand the strength of each company's balance sheet and compare their performance to others in the industry, according to a report from National Patient Account Services. A good BPO should focus on healthcare, have early-out services and use state-of-the-art technology to serve you.

HEALTHCARE BUSINESS IDEAS

If you're a healthcare professional or have an interest in working in the healthcare industry, there are plenty of different opportunities for you to start your own business. Some healthcare businesses require medical degrees while others have more specialized forms of training. There are also various certification requirements certain businesses. But for entrepreneurs who have the training, experience or aptitude, here are 50 different businesses you can start within the healthcare industry.

Healthcare Business Ideas

General Physician

When it comes to medical businesses, the first profession that comes to mind is a general doctor. Of course, you can work for a hospital or other medical facility. But you can also start your own practice or partnership if you want to have your own business.

Physical Therapist

With the right education and training, you can also start your own physical therapy practice where you help people recover after injury and offer other physical therapy services.

Dentist

Dental practices are often small, independent practices or partnerships. So that can be another very viable small business opportunity.

Optometrist

Or you can opt to help people maintain proper eye care and provide other vision related services as an optometrist.

Veterinarian

For those who would rather work with animals instead of people, starting a veterinary practice can be a viable business opportunity. But you do need a specialized degree in this field, of course.

Chiropractor

Chiropractors offer a variety of different services from basic adjustments to various forms of spine therapy.

Sleep Technician

Since many people experience issues with sleep, you can start a business that performs sleep tests and helps diagnose and treat patients experiencing some common sleep problems.

ObGyn

For a focus more on women's health and childbirth, you can train as an ObGyn and open a practice that might have a partnership with a local hospital for the actual deliveries.

Dermatologist

Dermatologists diagnose and treat skin issues. So you can start a practice offering those services to local patients who need help in that area.

Urgent Care Center Operator

Since many patients might need medical care without making an appointment days ahead of time but don't necessarily want to visit an emergency room, urgent care facilities can offer simple medical tests, diagnosis and treatment to those patients.

Pediatrician

If you specifically want to work with young patients, you can start your own practice as a pediatrician.

Concierge Doctor

Concierge doctors work on retainer for specific patients or organizations and often travel to their patients to provide care.

Doula

Doulas are professionals who provide various services to make the childbirth process easier and more comfortable for parents.

Midwife

Or you could train as a midwife, which is a more medically focused position that provides assistance to women during, before and after the childbirth process.

Herbalist

Herbal supplements and remedies can provide natural solutions to many different ailments. And you can build a business helping people get the herbal remedies that could benefit them.

Acupuncturist

Acupuncture is another alternative health solution. With some training, you can offer acupuncture services out of your own clinic or spa type business.

Massage Therapist

You can also get trained and certified as a massage therapist and start a business at your own location or even travel to work with clients.

Psychiatrist

On the mental health side, you can train as a psychiatrist who can diagnose and treat mental conditions using a variety of methods, including medication.

Psychologist

Psychologists do not prescribe medication to their patients. But they do help patients with a variety of mental health issues through other forms of therapy.

Clinical Social Worker

Clinical social work is a specialty practice that also deals with the mental health field. You can have a practice that assesses, diagnoses and treats a variety of behavioral and mental health conditions.

Mental Health Counselor

Counselors can also diagnose and treat a variety of mental health issues. But they also provide a variety of counseling services that often involve actually talking through problems.

Alcohol and Drug Abuse Counselor

You can also offer a specialty type of counseling when it comes to mental health. Addiction can be a huge issue, so there's plenty of opportunity to help people in that area through a counseling practice.

Family Therapist

Or you could focus on providing therapy to families or couples that deal with a variety of issues including addiction or mental health ailments.

Nutritionist

If you want to help people improve their nutritional intake and habits, you can build a business as a nutritionist.

Supplement Manufacturer

You can also produce and sell your own line of nutritional supplements to stores or even online, though you need to be sure your products comply with government requirements.

Independent Pharmacy Operator

Or you can sell supplements and medications from other providers out of your own independent retail pharmacy.

Fertility Clinic Operator

Fertility clinics provide a number of different services for individuals and couples trying to conceive. If you have the training and resources, you can open your own clinic for this purpose.

Blood Bank Operator

You can also start a blood or plasma bank that collects donations from people and distributes them to medical facilities when needed.

Medical Equipment Manufacturer

Hospitals, doctors' offices and other medical facilities need a huge variety of different supplies. So you can start a business that specializes in a certain type of medical supply and then sell items directly to those facilities.

Health Blogger

If you're knowledgeable about health related topics, you can start a blog or website aimed at offering advice or insights on certain areas of health or overall wellness.

Health Related Show or YouTube Channel Producer

Likewise, you can start your own show or YouTube channel to share your health related insights with a more video focused audience.

Health Podcaster

Or if audio is your format of choice, you can start a podcast related to health and wellness to share your insights.

Medical Journal or Publication Publisher

You can also start an journal or print publication that publishes articles or other content from medical and wellness professionals.

Wellness Coach

If you prefer working with people in more of a one-on-one setting, you can start a business as a wellness coach where you can provide advice and coaching on things like nutrition and fitness.

Orthopedic Supply Store Operator

For those who want to start a retail type of business, you can open a store for orthopedic accessories and supplies for consumers.

Medical Bookstore Owner

You can also open a bookstore, either in person or online, that specializes in selling medical and wellness related books and publications.

Scrubs Retailer

Doctors, nurses and plenty of other medical professionals wear scrubs to work. So you can open a store that sells those items for medical professionals.

Drug Testing Business

You can also open your own drug testing business that

works with companies and organizations to test for things like alcohol and drug use.

Medical Software Developer

Hospitals, doctors' offices and other medical facilities all need various software programs to function. So you can create your own software program and sell it to those medical facilities.

Medical Waste Disposal Provider

Medical waste is a huge issue for a lot of facilities. If you can recycle or dispose of the waste for those facilities, you can build an entire business around that service.

Medical Cleaning Business

You can also offer a cleaning service that specifically works with medical facilities that need really extensive and specific cleaning services.

Medical Coding Service

The medical industry has a lot of codes for different diagnosis, procedures and services. So you can build a business around coding information from various medical facilities.

Medical Marijuana Business

Medical marijuana is becoming a big industry in a lot of states. If you have the proper licenses, you can start a business producing it or selling it to patients.

Medical Transportation Provider

For people who need non-emergency transportation to medical appointments or facilities, you can start a service specifically to provide transportation to those patients.

Home Healthcare Assistant

If you're a healthcare professional, you can also provide in-home care to patients who need someone to look after them on a fairly regular basis.

Health Fair Organizer

The medical industry provides a lot of potential networking and product showcasing opportunities. If you enjoy putting together events, you can organize health fairs for members of the industry or consumers who are interested in health and wellness events.

Fitness Center Operator

For those who want to help others get in shape, you can open a fitness center that helps people create regular exercise routines through classes, exercise equipment or even personal training.

Weight Loss Clinic Operator

Or you could focus specifically on consumers who want to lose weight, offering consulting services to help people with their diets and fitness activities.

Childbirth Class Provider

You can also offer classes that teach expecting parents about the childbirth process or about helpful techniques like Lamaze.

Natural Remedy Supplier

If you want to provide natural healthcare solutions to consumers, you can open your own store or supplier network that deals with natural remedies or solutions.

CONCLUSION

Managers should be responsible and willing to go the extra mile to ensure a quality facility is being maintained at all times for patient care. For this reason, managers hold an important position in the healthcare industry. They are able to connect the business aspects of running the hospital with the medical expertise to form a crucial & reliable link. It is this vital bond that determines the success of the hospital thus formulating a medical service that patients can depend on.

www.ingramcontent.com/pod-product-compliance
Lightning Source LLC
Chambersburg PA
CBHW051348150726
48000CB00003B/1094